BLAZING
New Trails

PATHFINDER EDITION

By Dana Jensen and Peter Winkler

CONTENTS

Face of History. *This actor plays Sacagawea in the National Geographic movie* Lewis & Clark: Great Journey West.

WHO WAS SACAGAWEA?

By Dana Jensen

THE WIND WHIPPED through the girl's long hair. The horses were galloping fast, and she held on for dear life, not knowing where she was being taken. All she knew was that she was going farther and farther from her home.

A New Life

The girl was Sacagawea, a young Native American, and a member of the Shoshone people in Idaho.

A raiding party from another group kidnapped her when she was about 12. This was in or around the year 1800. After spending four years with them, she married a fur trader.

In 1804, she met Meriwether Lewis and William Clark, who were camping nearby for the winter. Meeting them changed her life.

President Thomas Jefferson had hired Lewis and Clark for an important **expedition**—to map out the West. They would travel to the Pacific Ocean, creating a team called the **Corps** of Discovery to do this.

They needed to find the best way to cross the country. They would meet Native Americans and travel through areas they had never seen.

Lewis and Clark knew Sacagawea would be helpful. Some of the lands on the journey belonged to the Shoshone, and she could speak their language and trade for horses.

Sacagawea's husband would also be a useful **interpreter**, so in 1805 Lewis and Clark hired the couple. Sacagawea, who was just 17 years old, was the only woman in the group.

Into the Wild

The team set out in April 1805. Sacagawea had just given birth to a son who traveled with them, strapped to his mother's back.

A month later, they were on the Missouri River when a fierce storm roared up. It tossed their boats around, nearly capsizing Sacagawea's boat and washing many of the team's tools and papers into the river.

Sacagawea sprang into action, retrieving the items from the water and saving valuable information from being lost forever.

Young Explorer. *Sacagawea's son accompanied her on the journey.*

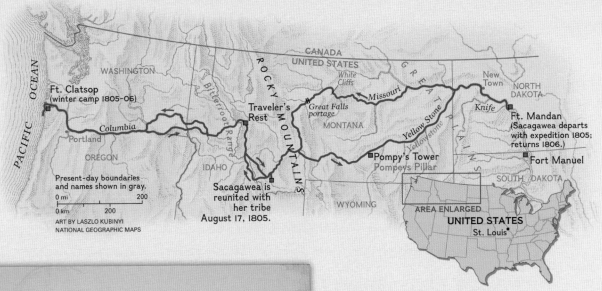

CANADA
UNITED STATES

Present-day boundaries
and names shown in gray.
0 mi   200

0 km   200

ART BY LASZLO KUBINYI
NATIONAL GEOGRAPHIC MAPS

Ft. Clatsop
(winter camp 1805-06)

PACIFIC OCEAN

WASHINGTON

Columbia

Portland

OREGON

IDAHO

Traveler's
Rest

ROCKY MOUNTAINS

Bitterroot Range

Sacagawea is
reunited with
her tribe
August 17, 1805.

White
Cliffs

Missouri

Great Falls
portage

MONTANA

Yellowstone

Yellowstone

Pompy's Tower
Pompeys Pillar

WYOMING

GREAT PLAINS

New
Town

Knife

NORTH
DAKOTA

Ft. Mandan
(Sacagawea departs
with expedition 1805;
returns 1806.)

Fort Manuel

SOUTH DAKOTA

AREA ENLARGED

UNITED STATES
St. Louis

TRAIL ❧ OF ❧ DISCOVERY

APRIL 1803: France sells the Louisiana Territory to the United States.

JULY 1803: President Thomas Jefferson hires Lewis and Clark to explore the new territory.

MAY 1804: Lewis and Clark leave St. Louis to begin the journey west.

APRIL 1805: Lewis and Clark ask Sacagawea to join the expedition.

AUGUST 1805: Sacagawea and her brother are reunited.

NOVEMBER 1805: The expedition reaches the Pacific Northwest.

MARCH 1806: The group starts the journey back home.

AUGUST 1806: Sacagawea returns to her home village.

SEPTEMBER 1806: Lewis and Clark end the expedition in St. Louis.

A Very Long Trip

In August 1805, the Corps reached the Shoshone, and Sacagawea quickly recognized the chief. He was her brother!

After they hugged and celebrated, Sacagawea traded with him. She got horses to help the Corps get through the steep mountains ahead.

After seven months and 4,000 kilometers (2,500 miles), the Corps neared the end of their journey. It was getting cold, and they needed a place to spend the winter. Everyone, including Sacagawea, voted on where they should stay.

They decided to build a camp, which they named Fort Clatsop, a few miles from the ocean. It was in an area that is now part of Oregon.

The winter was long and harsh, and they nearly ran out of food. Luckily, the group learned of a dead whale on a nearby beach, which would provide them with badly needed food and supplies.

Actors portray Lewis and Clark.

Sacagawea, wishing to see the ocean, asked to go with the men to look for the whale. This was the only time she asked for anything. The rest of the Corps let her go along with them.

Hard Hike.
Sacagawea never complained, and her strength impressed the men of the Corps.

Home, Sweet Home

In March 1806, the team began the long journey back home. On the way back, they passed through lands where Sacagawea had played as a child. Because she knew the area, she was able to help them find an easier route through the mountains.

After walking for sixteen months, Sacagawea, her son, and her husband arrived home, having traveled 8,000 kilometers (5,000 miles).

The trip had been grueling. They had crossed steep mountains, battled raging rivers, and survived fierce snowstorms.

Not much is known about Sacagawea's life after the expedition ended. She had a baby girl a short time later and probably died in her mid-20s.

During the trip, Clark had become fond of Sacagawea's son. After Sacagawea died, Clark took care of the boy and his sister. Clark called him Pomp, which is Shoshone for "leader."

Sacagawea's Legacy

Sacagawea was one of the reasons for the Corps' success. She was not only a symbol of peace to the Native Americans they encountered along the way, but she could also talk and trade with some groups. She helped to locate food when the Corps had nothing to eat.

Sacagawea's legend endures today. It is said there are more statues of her in the country than of any other American woman. She is a big part of American history, and we should all be proud of her. She was courageous and strong. We may not know much about her, but we know she is one of America's leading ladies.

WORDWISE

corps: a group of people working together on a project

expedition: trip taken for exploring

interpreter: person who tells what is being said in another language

Tale *from the* TRAIL

A Play by Peter Winkler

President Thomas Jefferson

The Lewis and Clark expedition is in for a big surprise. Relive it in this classroom play.

President Thomas Jefferson was a curious man. For years he had wanted to know about the lands west of the Mississippi River, so he asked Meriwether Lewis to lead an expedition, or special trip, to find out. Lewis teamed up with an old friend named William Clark.

Together they led a band of explorers from St. Louis all the way to the Pacific Ocean. Along the way, the group took on some new members. The most famous was a Shoshone (shuh SHOW nee) woman named Sacagawea (sak uh juh WEE uh).

The play takes place in August 1805. After traveling for more than a year, Lewis and Clark have reached the Bitterroot Mountains of Montana and Idaho.

"Gates of the Rocky Mountains." That's what Meriwether Lewis called the Montana landscape. His team canoed along this stretch of the Missouri River in July 1805. Lewis wrote that these were "the most remarkable [cliffs] that we have yet seen."

CHARACTERS

Cameahwait, *Shoshone chief*

Toussaint Charbonneau, *interpreter*

William Clark, *captain*

George Drouillard, *interpreter*

Jumping Fish, *Shoshone teen*

Meriwether Lewis, *captain*

Hugh McNeal, *soldier*

John Ordway, *sergeant*

Sacagawea, *Shoshone interpreter*

John Shields, *soldier*

Shoshone Woman

Shoshone Girl

SCENE 1: Big Job

(Lewis, Drouillard (dru YAR), Shields, and McNeal enter and stand on one side of the stage.)

Lewis: We have a big job, men. We must find some Indians—soon! Meanwhile, Captain Clark is leading the rest of our team up the river. We'll meet them again in a few days.

McNeal: We've met lots of Indians over the months. Why is it so important to meet more?

Lewis: Horses.

McNeal: I don't understand, captain.

Shields: Look at these rugged mountains! We need horses to carry our gear, and there's only one way to get horses.

Wild Ride. *Getting through the Rocky Mountains would be a challenge. The team couldn't haul all its gear on foot. What to do? The only answer was to meet the Indians and trade for horses.*

Drouillard: Trade with the Indians. If we can find them, that is.

(The explorers begin walking and looking around.)

McNeal: Sacagawea says that her people live nearby, doesn't she?

Lewis: Yes. They're called the Shoshone Indians. Of course, she hasn't seen them in four years—not since that raiding party kidnapped her.

Drouillard: Poor thing. She must have been terrified, and then wound up married to that French trader, Charbonneau (shahr buh NOH).

Shields: He's about as worthless as they get. I really can't believe he's part of our team.

Lewis: Watch your tongue!

Shields: I'm sorry, captain. At least he brought Sacagawea along. She's strong, and she's tough.

McNeal: I've never seen her show fear.

Drouillard: I've never seen her show any emotion.

Lewis: That's enough chatter. If there are Indians around, we don't want to scare them away. I doubt the Shoshone have ever met white people, and they might think we're their enemies.

(The explorers walk silently and continue looking around. Meanwhile, a Shoshone woman and girl enter. They stand at a distance, watching carefully.)

SCENE 2: First Contact

(The Shoshone whisper to each other.)

Shoshone Girl: Those are not our people.

Shoshone Woman: No. I don't recognize them.

Shoshone Girl: Have they come to attack us?

Shoshone Woman: I don't know. Sit down and stay still, and maybe they won't see us.

(The Shoshone sit with arms crossed and heads bowed. Lewis soon spots them, and he and his men stop. They whisper.)

Lewis: Do you see them?

Others: Yes.

Lewis: Wait here. I'm going to them—slowly. McNeal, hand me the flag. Shields, find me some beads.

(Shields hangs some beads around Lewis's neck, and McNeal gives him a small U.S. flag. Lewis unfolds it and holds it up as he inches forward.)

Lewis: I am not an enemy—I've come to trade.

(Lewis repeats those sentences until he reaches the Indians. Then he gently touches the woman's arm and nudges her to stand. The girl watches, and then stands, too. Lewis gives them each a string of beads.)

Lewis: Greetings! My name is Meriwether Lewis, and I am not an enemy. I am your friend.

Shoshone Girl: You are?

Lewis: Yes. My people live far to the east. Our Great Father, Thomas Jefferson, sent me to explore this land.

Shoshone Girl: What do you want with us?

Lewis: I would like to meet your chief.

Shoshone Woman: Well, you didn't hurt or kill us, so I'll take a risk and trust you. Come meet our people.

(Lewis waves his men over, and everyone exits together.)

SCENE 3: Where Are They?

(Clark, Charbonneau, Ordway, Sacagawea, and any extra explorers enter. They mime paddling canoes as they move slowly across stage. Through it all, Sacagawea is stone-faced.)

Charbonneau: I'm tired. I'm so tired. Can't we stop for a few minutes?

Ordway: You lazy lump of stone! You do nothing but complain. Your wife does more work than you do.

Charbonneau: Shut your mouth, Ordway! I'm not one of your soldiers.

Ordway: That's for sure. You'd never—*(Clark interrupts.)*

Clark: That's enough, you two! Shut your mouths and open your eyes. Captain Lewis should be around here somewhere—it's been almost a week since he went ahead.

Charbonneau: Yes, captain.

Ordway: Sorry, captain.

(Clark takes out a spyglass and peers over the landscape.)

Peace Offering. *After days of searching, Meriwether Lewis met two Shoshone Indians on August 13, 1805. He gave them beads and other gifts—symbols of peace and friendship.*

Clark: I see people, but I can't tell who they are. Let's move quickly.

(Everyone paddles quickly.)

Ordway: I see them now. There's Shields and McNeal.

Sacagawea: And that's Captain Lewis.

Clark: Looks like he's found some Indians. I hope they'll trade with us. *(Sacagawea opens her eyes wide and smiles broadly.)*

Clark: What is it?

Sacagawea: Those are— Those are—

Charbonneau: What, what?! Out with it!

Sacagawea: Those—are—my—people.

(Everyone stops paddling and comes ashore.)

SCENE 4: Remember Me?

(Clark and his group stand still. Lewis and his men walk toward them. So do Cameahwait (KAH moh wait), Jumping Fish, and any Shoshone extras. The captains shout to each other.)

Lewis: Captain Clark!

Clark: Captain Lewis!

Lewis: All well?

Clark: Yes. And you?

Lewis: Yes indeed.

(Looking hard at Sacagawea, Jumping Fish leaps excitedly. Then she runs forward.)

Jumping Fish: Sacagawea! Is it you? Is it really you?

Sacagawea: Yes, yes!

Jumping Fish: I never thought I'd see you again.

(The two embrace.)

McNeal: What are they doing?

Cameahwait: Four years ago, the two girls were kidnapped. One escaped by leaping into a river, so we call her Jumping Fish.

(As both groups come together, Shoshone and explorers embrace. The explorers give beads and mirrors to the Shoshone.)

Lewis: I hope our peoples will be friends for years to come.

Clark: We can both benefit by trading.

Cameahwait: We wish to trade. You need horses, and you may have things we can use.

(Sacagawea stares at Cameahwait. Then she races toward him and greets him.)

Drouillard: Now what?

Jumping Fish: Our chief is Sacagawea's brother. You have brought them together again.

Sacagawea: My people. My family. I ached for this moment, but I never dared to hope for it.

Cameahwait: Sorrow has become joy. Welcome home, sister. Welcome and thanks, new friends.

(Everyone bows.)

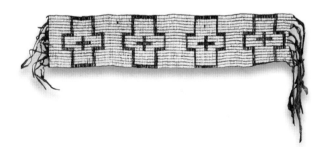

Famous Face. *In 2000, Sacagawea's accomplishments were honored with a dollar coin.*

10

AMAZING PEOPLE
AMAZING EXPEDITION

Read their files to find out why.

WILLIAM CLARK

BORN: August 1, 1770, in Caroline County, Virginia

KNOWLEDGE AND SKILLS:
mapmaking, river navigation, negotiating with Indians

CAREER HIGHLIGHTS:
joined frontier militia (1789); retired as officer, U.S. Army (1796);
led expedition to Pacific Northwest with Meriwether Lewis (1804–06);
superintendent of Indian Affairs (1808–38);
published expedition journals (1814);
governor of the Missouri Territory (1813–21)

DIED: September 1, 1838, in St. Louis, Missouri

MERIWETHER LEWIS

BORN: August 18, 1774, near Charlottesville, Virginia

KNOWLEDGE AND SKILLS:
natural history, medicine, geography, and writing

CAREER HIGHLIGHTS:
joined U.S. Army (1794), became captain (1800);
private secretary to President Thomas Jefferson (1801);
led expedition to Pacific Northwest with William Clark (1804–06);
governor of the Louisiana Territory (1807)

DIED: October 10, 1809, near Nashville, Tennessee

SACAGAWEA

BORN: c. 1788, in the Lemhi River valley, near the present-day border between Idaho and Montana

KNOWLEDGE AND SKILLS:
Shoshone interpreter, knowledge of edible plants and foraging techniques, knowledge of landmarks, symbol of expedition's peaceful intentions

CAREER HIGHLIGHTS:
captured by a Hidatsa raiding party and taken to North Dakota (about 1800); married Toussaint Charbonneau (about 1804); gave birth to a son, Jean Baptiste (February 11, 1805); joined expedition to Pacific Northwest (April 7, 1805); saved Clark's journals when boat nearly capsized (May 14, 1805); reunited with brother Cameahwait, which enabled expedition to continue across the Rocky Mountains (mid-August 1805); saw the Pacific Ocean (November 1805)

DIED: December 20, 1812?, at Fort Manuel, on the Missouri River, in present-day South Dakota

Crossing New
FRONTIERS

**Follow Sacagawea's example. Blaze new
trails to answer these questions.**

1 What was the purpose of Lewis and
Clark's expedition?

2 Who was Sacagawea?

3 At the beginning of the play,
why does Lewis want to find
Native Americans?

4 How did Sacagawea's relationship
with the Shoshone chief
Cameahwait help the expedition?

5 What skills did Sacagawea bring to
the Corps of Discovery? How were
Lewis and Clark's skills different?